A huge bird swoops down.

In the blink of an eye, it snatches a fish from the waters below, then flies away.

BALD EAGLES

GAIL GIBBONS

HOLIDAY HOUSE NEW YORK

This book was first published as *Soaring with the Wind* in 1998 by Morrow Junior Books, a division of William Morrow and Company.
HOLIDAY HOUSE is registered in the U.S. Patent and Trademark Office.
Printed and bound in December 2025 at Toppan Leefung, DongGuan, China.
www.holidayhouse.com
First Holiday House Edition
10 9 8 7 6 5 4 3 2 1
ISBN: 978-0-8234-6288-9 (hardcover)
The Library of Congress has cataloged the prior edition as follows:
Gibbons, Gail. Soaring with the wind: the bald eagle/Gail Gibbons. p cm. Summary: Describes the characteristics, behavior, and life cycle of the bald eagle. ISBN 0-688-13731-8 (library) 1. Bald eagle—Juvenile literature. [1. Bald eagle. 2. Eagles.] I. Title QL696.F32G5 1998 598.9'43—dc21 97-20497 CIP AC
EU Authorized Representative: HackettFlynn Ltd, 36 Cloch Choirneal, Balrothery, Co. Dublin, K32 C942, Ireland.
EU@walkerpublishinggroup.com

To Rebecca and Eric, my grown-up children

The author wishes to thank Peter Nye, research scientist with the New York State Division of Fish and Wildlife, Delma, New York, for his expert help. Thanks also to Mike Owen of the Fakahatchee Strand State Preserve, Copeland, Florida.

The publisher would like to thank Paul Sweet, Collection Manager, Department of Ornithology, American Museum of Natural History, for his expert review of the text.

The Bald Eagle is a *raptor*. Raptors are birds of prey, which means they eat meat. The name *raptor* comes from the Latin word *rapere*, meaning “to grasp or seize by force.” Bald Eagles are excellent hunters, gripping their prey with claws, also called *talons*, that are razor-sharp and four inches long.

A Bald Eagle isn't bald. Its name comes from *balde*, an Old English word meaning "white." With its gleaming white head and tail feathers, the Bald Eagle is instantly recognizable. It belongs to the group of eagles called *fish and sea eagles* that lives near water and eats mostly fish and water birds.

An adult Bald Eagle is about three feet tall from head to tail and weighs about eleven pounds. The female is bigger than the male. They both have the same basic characteristics.

A thin, clear eyelid called the NICTITATING (NICK-tah-tate-ing) membrane protects and cleans the eye.

The Bald Eagle is one of the largest hunting birds in North America. Its body is perfectly designed for flight and catching prey. The entire skeleton of a Bald Eagle weighs only about half a pound. Each bone is hollow and filled with air.

There are about 7,000 feathers on a Bald Eagle's body. Together, they weigh a little less than one and a half pounds. They overlap one another to create a lot of air space in between. This helps to *insulate*, or protect, the bird's body from heat and cold.

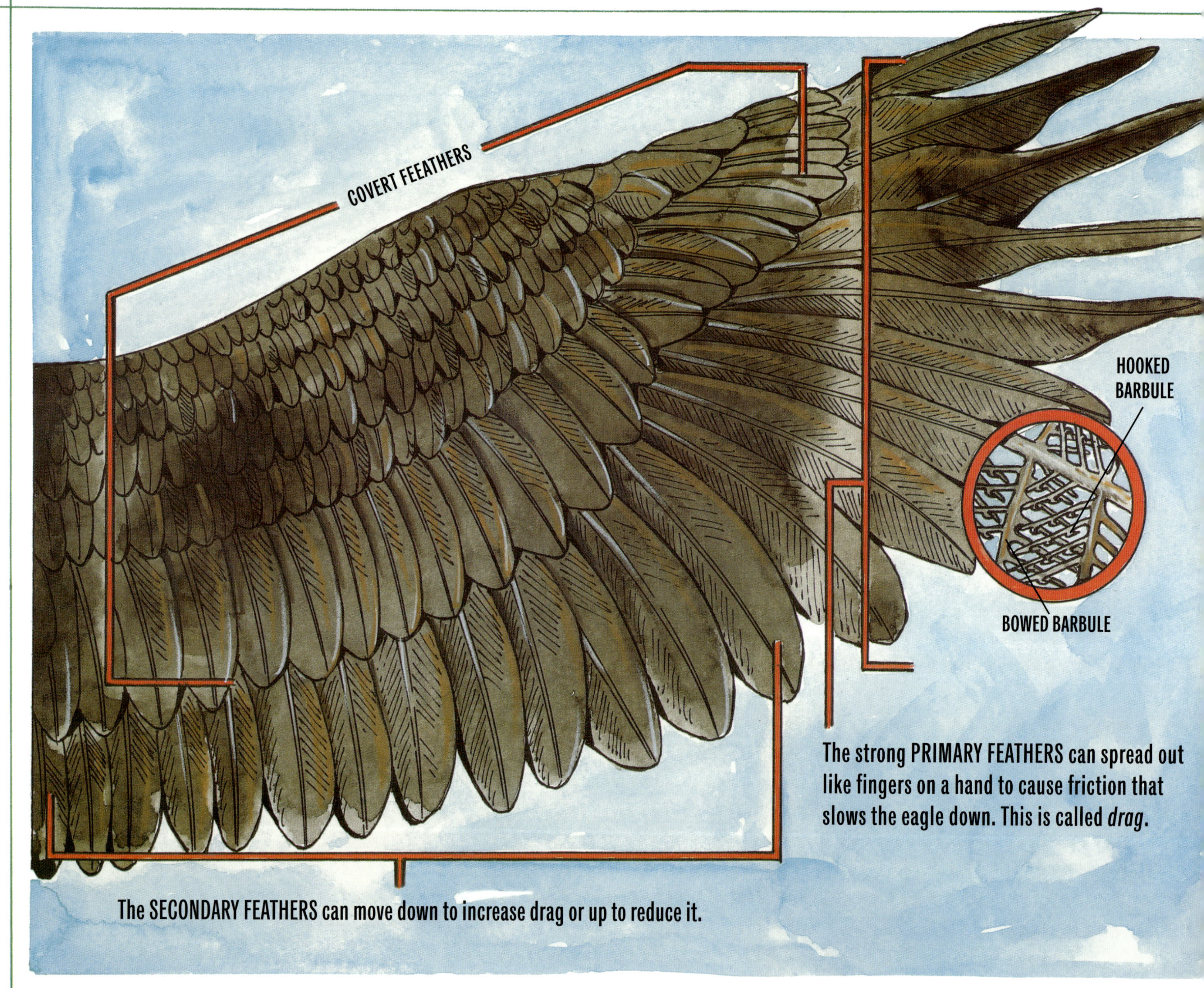
COVERT FEEATHERS
HOOKED BARBULE
BOWED BARBULE
The strong PRIMARY FEATHERS can spread out like fingers on a hand to cause friction that slows the eagle down. This is called *drag*.
The SECONDARY FEATHERS can move down to increase drag or up to reduce it.

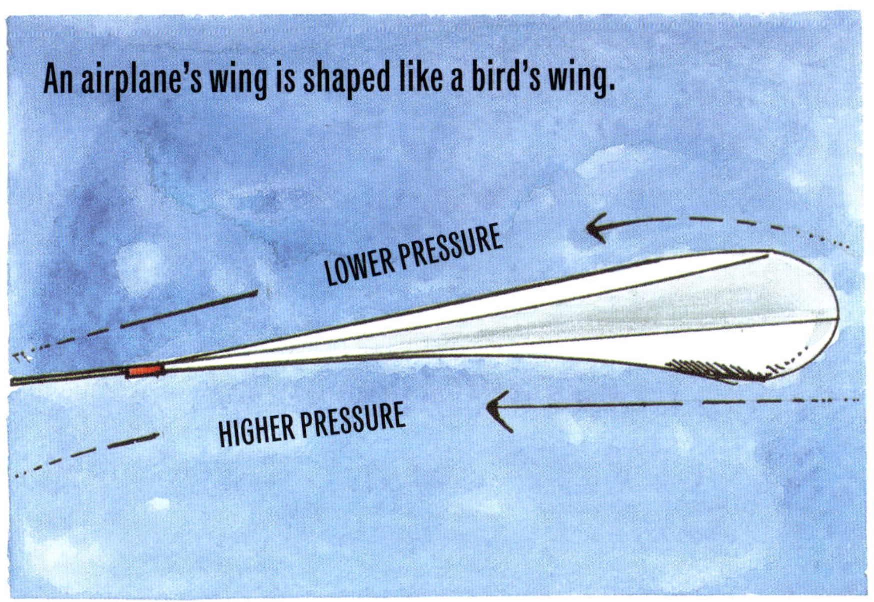

The feathers are strong because they are made of *keratin*, just like your fingernails. Each feather is held together by a pattern of *barbules*. More than 350,000 tiny *hooked barbules* are attached to *bowed barbules* to give each feather its particular shape.

Like most birds, eagles are streamlined for flight. Their wingspan can be as wide as seven and a half feet. Their wings are flatter on the bottom than on top, just like an airplane's wings. The Bald Eagle uses its wing feathers to lift off and change direction, and it can dive down through the air at 100 miles an hour!

When the Bald Eagle wants to soar far up into the sky, it often hitches a ride on rising hot-air currents called *thermals*. Once it gets into the thermal, the eagle spreads its long and narrow wings and floats like a hang glider. Sometimes a really big thermal can carry an eagle three miles above the earth!

When the sun warms the ground, the air above it rises. These rising warm-air currents are called THERMALS.

RESOLVING POWER is the ability to focus on things far away. A Bald Eagle has eight times more resolving power than a person.

Eagles only kill when they are hungry. Their yellow eyes have amazing vision that can see objects up to two miles away. They can hear faraway sounds too, like the splash of a fish. When an eagle finds its prey, it can spread its wings and float down so quietly that its victim can't hear it coming.

SPICULES, tiny spikes on the toes, help hold slippery prey.

A Bald Eagle can eat four to five fish a day. They also eat birds, rabbits, other small creatures, and the carcasses of dead animals. The Bald Eagle is so strong, it can lift half its own body weight. Its sharp talons dig into and kill what it catches. Then it shreds and tears its prey apart with its sharp, hook-shaped beak so its meal is easy to eat. Each eagle has its own hunting ground and may attack another eagle coming into its territory.

Bald Eagles are found only in North America. Some eagles live and hunt in the same area all year-round, but most migrate when the seasons change. When winter sets in and snow and ice cover the land and waters, many northern eagles fly south until they find open water and prey. In the spring, they return to their breeding grounds in the north. This traveling back and forth is called *migration*. Some eagles migrate thousands of miles.

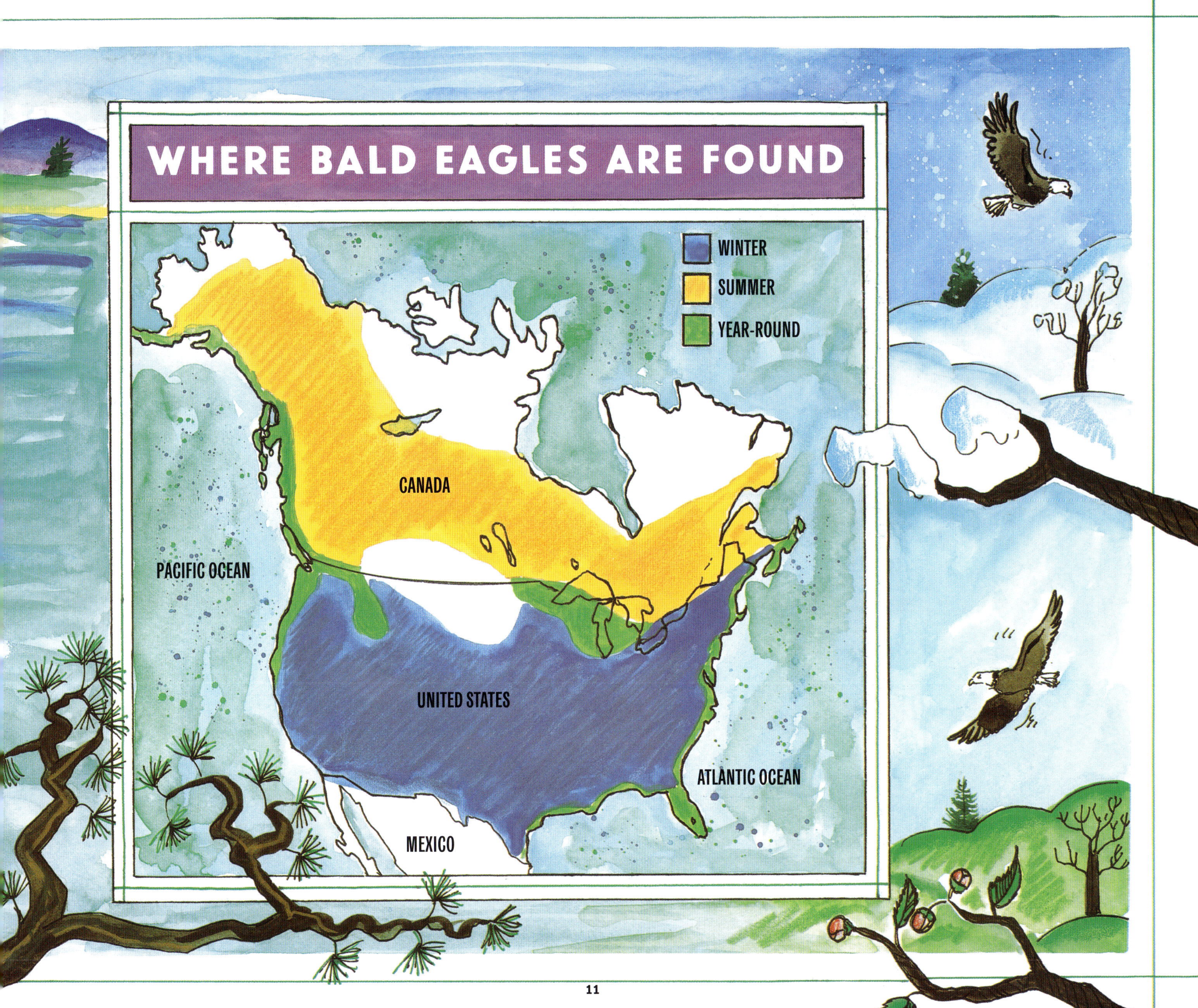
WHERE BALD EAGLES ARE FOUND
WINTER
SUMMER
YEAR-ROUND
CANADA
PACIFIC OCEAN
UNITED STATES
ATLANTIC OCEAN
MEXICO

Spring is mating season. Male and female eagles attract each other with a high-pitched call. They usually mate for life. They take a new mate only when their first mate dies. Once they've mated, eagles return to the same nesting territory year after year.

Before mating, there is a fascinating form of behavior called the *courtship ritual*. Some of it takes place in the air. A male and female chase each other, dive, and make loops. Sometimes, high in the sky, they lock their talons together and cartwheel downward. Just before touching ground, they let go and fly upward again. During the spring, some eagles spend more time and energy courting than hunting.

After courtship and mating, nest-building begins. Bald Eagles build the largest nests of any bird. Most are about six feet deep and six feet in diameter. A new nesting pair builds its nest in a high, out-of-reach place, almost always in a tree. They weave twigs and large sticks together and line the nest with soft mosses, feathers, leaves, and grasses. Pairs that have been mates before add to and clean up their old nests. They build a new nest only if their old one has fallen down.

The nest is called an AERIE (AIR-EE).

Female Bald Eagles lay one to three eggs. The male and female take turns sitting on the eggs to keep them warm. Brooding time has begun. This is called *incubation*. While one sits on the eggs, its mate hunts for food and fiercely guards the nesting territory from intruders.

After about thirty-five days, a peep comes from inside an egg. A chick is ready to hatch. It uses its *egg tooth* to peck its way out of the shell. This tiring struggle can take from a few hours to two days. Finally, the chick appears. The chick, called an *eaglet*, weighs about three ounces. It is helpless, wet, and tiny. One by one, the other eggs hatch.

EAGLET

The parents care for and feed the eaglets. One parent keeps them warm while the other hunts. The parents use their beaks to tear apart meat into pieces small enough for the eaglets to eat. These eaglets are two days old and covered in dry, fluffy down.

After about one month, the eaglets have lost their first coat of down. Their new coat is thick and woolly. The eaglets are about ten times bigger than when they were born. When they are around two months old, their feathers have grown in. They practice flying by hopping up and down and hovering in the air. Their parents continue to feed and care for them.

Now they are four months old and fully grown. They fly out of the nest, gliding to nearby branches. Flying for the first time is called *fledging*. For the next two months, the eaglets, now called *fledglings*, will stay with their parents and master their hunting skills.

In the fall, many young eagles, now called *immatures*, fly south to join other migrating Bald Eagles. It will take about five years for them to develop the brilliant white head and tail feathers, as well as the bright yellow eyes, of their parents. Then they will be ready to mate and raise their own young.

Because of the fierce strength and beauty of the Bald Eagle, it has been a symbol in North America for centuries. Many Indigenous Peoples revere these birds, viewing them as sacred. In some Indigenous cultures, it is said the Bald Eagle carries prayers to the Creator.

To many Indigenous Peoples, the Bald Eagle plays an important role spiritually and culturally. Bald Eagle feathers are sometimes used in ceremonies, given as a gift of honor, or featured in art. Some Native Peoples and Nations of the Pacific Northwest Coast carve totem poles that feature Bald Eagles. It is very important to protect Bald Eagles and their habitat.

In 1782, the Bald Eagle was chosen by the Continental Congress as the emblem of the United States of America. It represents strength, dignity, and freedom. Its image is found on coins, flags, monuments, and many other objects.

Once there were thousands of Bald Eagles in North America. Then people began hunting them for sport. Farmers shot them because they falsely believed Bald Eagles killed small farm animals and too many fish. Also, people moved into wilderness areas, cutting down trees and destroying the eagles' territory.

Then farmers sprayed their fields with a poison called DDT to protect their crops from pests. Rainwater carried the DDT into waterways, poisoning fish and other sources of the Bald Eagles' food. When eagles fed on prey that was contaminated with DDT, some died. Others laid eggs that never hatched because DDT had made the eggshells so thin and soft.

In 1969, only a few hundred pairs of these birds were left in the lower forty-eight states. So the United States added the Bald Eagle to the nation's endangered species list. *Endangered* means "in danger of becoming *extinct*." The government created laws to protect Bald Eagles, and it set aside land, called *sanctuaries*, where it is safe for Bald Eagles to live. Now it is illegal to kill or even disturb a Bald Eagle.

In 1972, the use of DDT in the United States was banned, and in 1976, a number of state and private wildlife organizations began programs to restore eagles to the land. Eaglets are raised by humans in a safe natural environment that will eventually be their home—a process called *hacking*.

EXTINCT means "to no longer exist."

HACK TOWER

The number of Bald Eagles has steadily increased over time as a result of these efforts. While they are no longer endangered, Bald Eagles still need to be protected. Today, global warming is a threat. If human beings can maintain safe and adequate places for them to live—which is the most important thing humans can do—Bald Eagles will go on being warriors of the sky.

WARRIORS OF THE SKY

There are sixty-one kinds of eagles in the world. They are found on every continent except Antarctica.

Falconers—people who train hawks for hunting—keep the birds in a state of partial liberty, called *at hack*, as they are being trained. The efforts of today's restoration programs are often known as *hacking*.

The largest Bald Eagle nest ever seen weighed about 2,000 pounds, as much as a car.

Some scientists and other people keep track of Bald Eagles by putting bands on the birds' legs. They want to make sure the eagle population continues to rise. These bands have different numbers on them to identify the different birds.

The term *eagle-eyed* means "to have good vision and notice things quickly."

Bald Eagles often catch weak and sick animals. That keeps the small-animal population healthy and our natural world in balance.

In the United States, the first image of a Bald Eagle appeared on a document signed by George Washington after the Revolutionary War.

In the wild, a Bald Eagle can live to be about forty years old. The adult eagle has no enemy except for people.

WARNING!

Never approach the nest of a Bald Eagle. This may cause the birds to flee, leaving their eggs to grow cold. Watch them from far away with binoculars. They don't like to be disturbed.